TRAVEL WITH THE GREAT EXPLORERS

Explore with

James Cook

Lisa Dalrymple

Crabtree Publishing Company
www.crabtreebooks.com

Crabtree Publishing Company
www.crabtreebooks.com

Author: Lisa Dalrymple
Publishing plan research
    and development: Reagan Miller
Managing Editor: Tim Cooke
Designer: Lynne Lennon
Picture Manager: Sophie Mortimer
Design Manager: Keith Davis
Editorial Director: Lindsey Lowe
Editor: Kelly Spence
Proofreader: Crystal Sikkens
Children's Publisher: Anne O'Daly
Production coordinator
    and prepress technician: Tammy McGarr
Print coordinator: Margaret Amy Salter

Produced by Brown Bear Books for
Crabtree Publishing Company

Photographs:
Front Cover: National Maritime Museum: RHL main; Shutterstock:
br, Regien Paassen cr, Photoslayer tr.

Interior: Bonhams: 12b; Bridgeman Art Library: De Agostini
Picture Library 10; Library of Congress: 11b, 19b, 29br; NASA: 14b;
National Maritime Museum: 28b; National Museum of Canada:
4–5b; National Museum of New Zealand: 4t; National Portrait
Gallery: 11t; Robert Hunt Library: 11br, Jeni Foto 28t, Racklever 15b;
Science & Society Picture Library: Florilgius 24b; Shutterstock: 7t,
13b, 14l, BMCL 12t, Neil Burton 17b, Barry Kearney 23t, Alberto
Loyo 5t, Photoslayer 22b, Randy Schafer 7b; Swaen.com: 27t;
Thinkstock: Jason Field 6bl, istockphoto 16b, 16br, 20–21t, Noblige
6–7, Jain Sourabh 29bl, Paul Wolf 25b; Topfoto: Barry Batchelor 16t,
British Library Board 18b, 20, The Granger Collection 17c, 18t, 22t,
23b, 25t, 27b, Liszt Collection 19l, Ann Ronan Picture Library 24t,
Topham Picturepoint 13t, 26t, 29t, ullsteinbild 21br, 26b
All other artwork and maps, Brown Bear Books Ltd.

Brown Bear Books has made every attempt to contact the
copyright holder. If you have any information please contact
licensing@brownbearbooks.co.uk

Library and Archives Canada Cataloguing in Publication

Dalrymple, Lisa, author
        Explore with James Cook / Lisa Dalrymple.

(Travel with the great explorers)
Includes index.
Issued in print and electronic formats.
ISBN 978-0-7787-1701-0 (bound).--
ISBN 978-0-7787-1705-8 (paperback).--
ISBN 978-1-4271-7708-7 (pdf).--ISBN 978-1-4271-7701-8 (html)

        1. Cook, James, 1728-1779--Juvenile literature. 2. Voyages
around the world--Juvenile literature. 3. Explorers--Great Britain-
-Biography--Juvenile literature. I. Title. II. Series: Travel with the
great explorers

G246.C7D35 2015   j910.92   C2015-903204-0
                                                        C2015-903205-9

Library of Congress Cataloging-in-Publication Data

Dalrymple, Lisa.
 Explore with James Cook / Lisa Dalrymple.
        pages cm. -- (Travel with the great explorers)
 Includes index.
 ISBN 978-0-7787-1701-0 (reinforced library binding : alk. paper) --
ISBN 978-0-7787-1705-8 (paperback : alk. paper) --
ISBN 978-1-4271-7708-7 (electronic PDF) --
ISBN 978-1-4271-7701-8 (electronic HTML)
 1. Cook, James, 1728-1779--Juvenile literature. 2. Explorers--Great
Britain--Biography--Juvenile literature. 3. Voyages around the world--
Juvenile literature. I. Title.

 G420.C65D35 2016
 910.92--dc23
 [B]
                                        2015021130

Crabtree Publishing Company

www.crabtreebooks.com   1-800-387-7650

Printed in Canada/082015/BF20150630

Published in Canada
Crabtree Publishing
616 Welland Ave.
St. Catharines, ON
L2M 5V6

Published in the United States
Crabtree Publishing
PMB 59051
350 Fifth Avenue, 59th Floor
New York, New York 10118

Published in the United Kingdom
Crabtree Publishing
Maritime House
Basin Road North, Hove
BN41 1WR

Published in Australia
Crabtree Publishing
3 Charles Street
Coburg North
VIC, 3058

CONTENTS

Meet the Boss

Did you know?

Cook was promoted quickly after he joined the Royal Navy. He became a full ship's master after only two years. That meant he could command his own vessels.

In the 1700s, explorer James Cook set sail to claim new lands for Britain. On his three voyages of exploration, Cook charted unexplored waters with such detail that his maps continued to be used into the 20th century.

HUMBLE BEGINNINGS

+ Coal-carrying captain has ambitions

James Cook was born in 1728 in northern England as the son of a farm worker. Cook was good at math, so his father's employer paid for him to go school. When he grew up, Cook went to sea on coal ships from the port of Whitby. He learned about **navigation** and astronomy. Although he was offered his own ship to command, Cook was now determined to join the Royal Navy, Britain's military fleet. That meant starting all over again in the lower **ranks**.

IN THE NAVY

★ **Fighting the French—in Canada!**

As a ship's master in the Royal Navy, Cook's first posting was in Canada. British colonists were fighting the French and their native allies in the Seven Years' War (1756–1763). Cook mapped the coasts and rivers of Canada to help British sailors. The war ended with Britain defeating the French and capturing the cities of Montreal and Quebec.

★ **The Royal Navy made Cook keep his destinations secret, even from his crew. They wanted to prevent other countries from interfering with British claims to new territory. Would you go on a voyage if you didn't know the destination? Explain your reasoning for or against.**

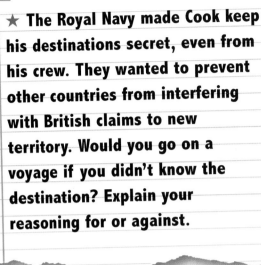

SURVEYING THE LAND

☛ **Master mapper gets to work**

Cook's mathematical talent made him a skilled navigator and mapmaker. After the British victory in the Seven Years' War, Cook charted the coasts of Britain's new Canadian territory in Newfoundland and Labrador. He became known as one of the best **surveyors** of his time.

A FAMILY MAN

★ **Explorer has six children**

★ **Son follows father to sea**

In 1762, Cook married Elizabeth Batts. Her father owned an inn near the docks in London. The couple had six children: James, Nathaniel, Elizabeth, Joseph, George, and Hugh. Only James, Nathaniel, and Hugh survived childhood. Nathaniel followed his father and went to sea. He died at age 16, when his ship sank during a hurricane in the Caribbean Sea.

Where Are We Heading?

Cook made three voyages of discovery. Each lasted about three years. Cook was the first European to reach many places and he made maps everywhere he went.

Did you know?

In 1769, Cook sailed from Tahiti and claimed New Zealand for Britain. He sailed around the entire island and made maps for future sailors.

PACIFIC ISLAND

- ☞ Explorers observes planet
- ☞ Swears to return

In 1768, Cook began his first voyage of discovery. The Royal Navy hired him to sail to the island of Tahiti in the Pacific Ocean. He was to record the **transit** of Venus, which is when the planet passes across the face of the Sun. During his years at sea, Cook returned to Tahiti many times.

"AN INSANE LABYRINTH"

+ Cook gets stuck in vast reef

In 1770, on his first voyage, Cook landed in eastern Australia and named it New South Wales. While mapping Australia's east coast the ship *Endeavour* ran aground on the Great Barrier Reef. Cook called the reef "an insane **labyrinth**" of rocks and **coral**. He and his crew were stranded for three months while they made repairs to the ship.

COLD AS ICE!

Some scientists thought there was a "great southern continent" at the South Pole. In 1772, on his second voyage, Cook set out to find it. His ships sailed into the Southern Ocean. He found land—Antarctica. It was a southern continent, but it was ice-covered and uninhabitable.

HAWAII

Cook passed small Hawaiian Islands on his way to the Arctic. On the way back, he landed on the big island of Hawaii. He was killed there in February 1779.

TRAVEL UPDATE

The Closed Passage

★ If you're setting out to sail around the north of Canada, think again. In 1778, on his third voyage, Cook headed north to Alaska to search for the **Northwest Passage**. In theory, this route followed the top of Canada from the Pacific Ocean to the Atlantic Ocean. But Cook decided that there was no useful route because the sea was frozen solid most of the year.

EASTER ISLAND

★ World's most remote island

★ Watched over by giant heads

After sailing past the Antarctic, Cook headed north. He wanted to map Easter Island in the south Atlantic Ocean. The island was nearly deserted, but Cook did find mysterious stone statues erected by an ancient civilization.

JAMES COOK'S VOYAGES OF DISCOVERY

James Cook made three long voyages of discovery around the world. Most of his discoveries were made in the Pacific Ocean, but he also explored the northwestern North American coast.

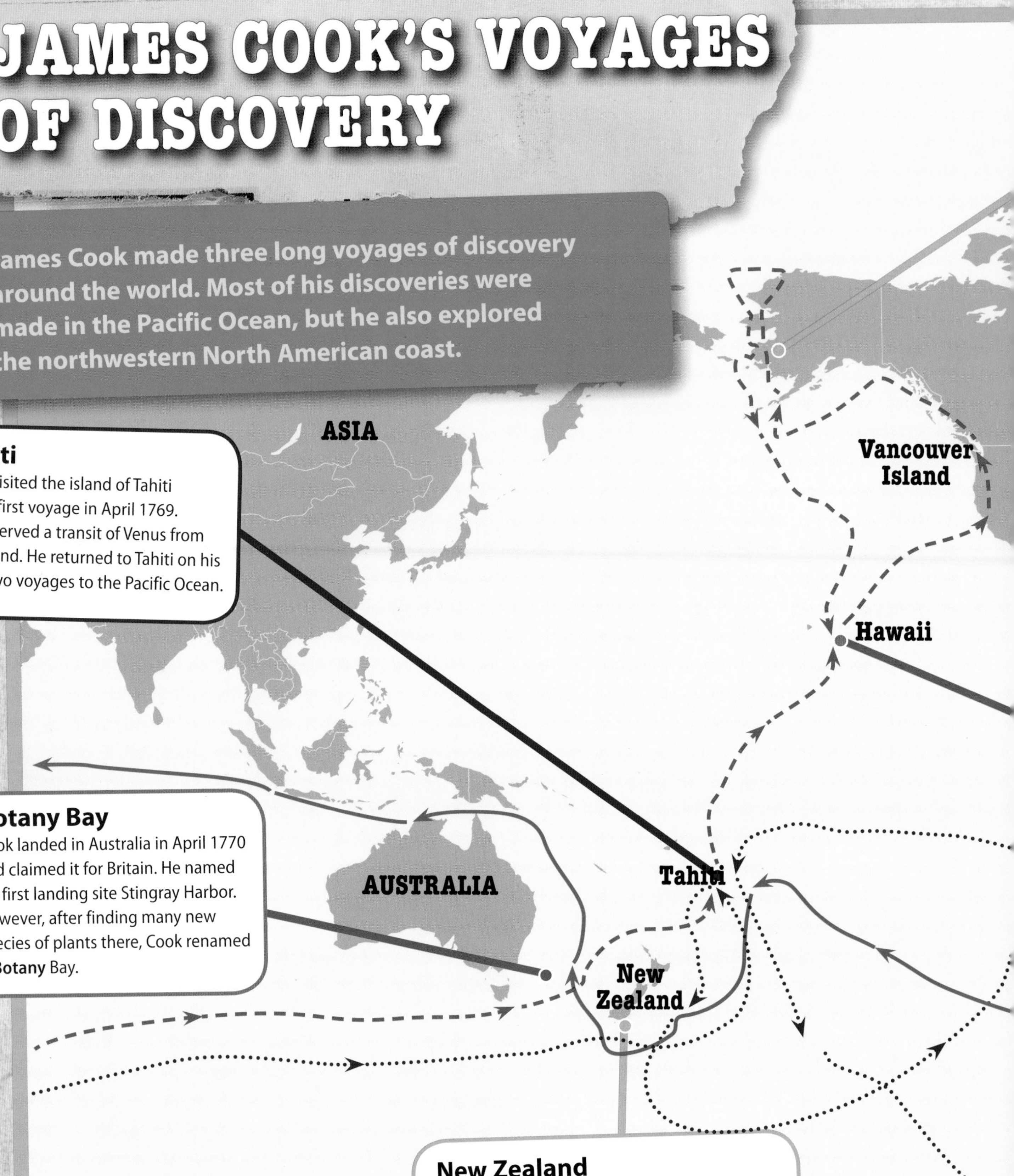

ASIA

Vancouver Island

Hawaii

Tahiti
Cook visited the island of Tahiti on his first voyage in April 1769. He observed a transit of Venus from the island. He returned to Tahiti on his next two voyages to the Pacific Ocean.

Botany Bay
Cook landed in Australia in April 1770 and claimed it for Britain. He named his first landing site Stingray Harbor. However, after finding many new species of plants there, Cook renamed it **Botany** Bay.

AUSTRALIA

Tahiti

New Zealand

New Zealand
On his first voyage in 1769, Cook charted the coast of New Zealand so accurately that the New Zealand navy continued to use his charts for centuries to come.

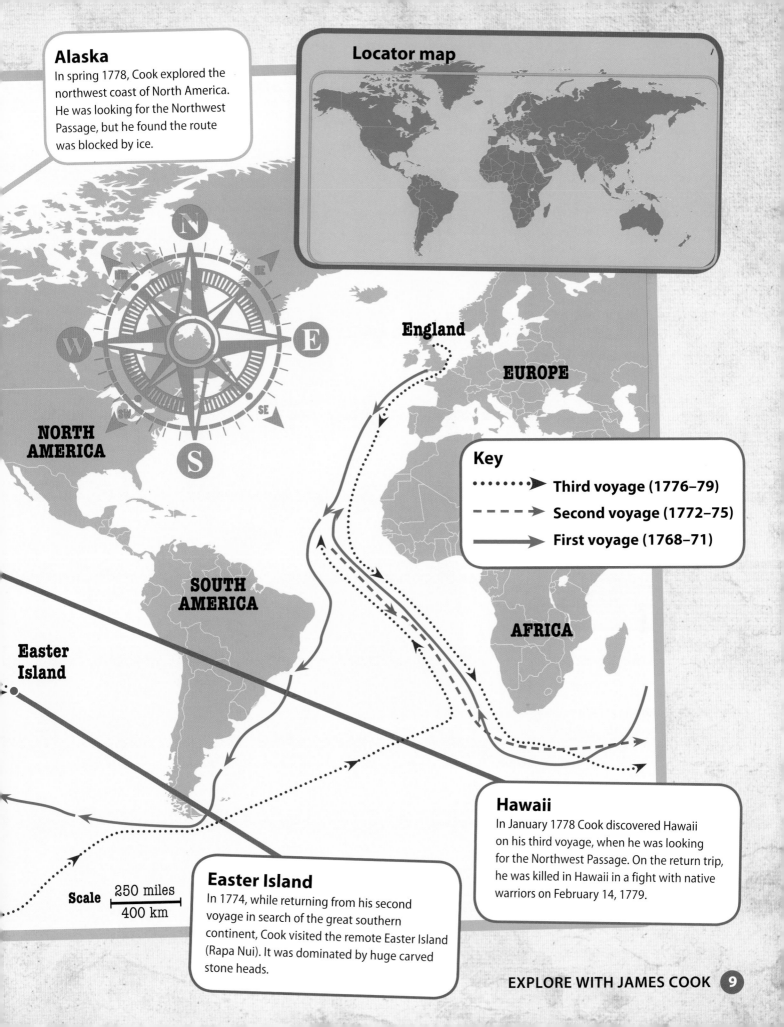

Alaska

In spring 1778, Cook explored the northwest coast of North America. He was looking for the Northwest Passage, but he found the route was blocked by ice.

Locator map

England

EUROPE

NORTH AMERICA

SOUTH AMERICA

AFRICA

Easter Island

Key

········➤ **Third voyage (1776–79)**

– – –➤ **Second voyage (1772–75)**

——➤ **First voyage (1768–71)**

Hawaii

In January 1778 Cook discovered Hawaii on his third voyage, when he was looking for the Northwest Passage. On the return trip, he was killed in Hawaii in a fight with native warriors on February 14, 1779.

Easter Island

In 1774, while returning from his second voyage in search of the great southern continent, Cook visited the remote Easter Island (Rapa Nui). It was dominated by huge carved stone heads.

Scale 250 miles / 400 km

Meet the Crew

Cook sailed with many different people, including navigators, scientists, and even a Tahitian priest. Some even tried to steal the credit for Cook's achievements.

CHARLES CLERKE

+ Cook's right-hand man

+ Brings ships home after captain's death

Charles Clerke was a good sailor and an entertaining storyteller. He sailed on all three of Cook's voyages. By the last journey, when Cook captained the *Resolution*, Clerke had learned enough from Cook to captain the *Discovery*. After Cook was killed in Hawaii in 1779, Clerke took command of the expedition. He sailed north in a second attempt to find the Northwest Passage. He died of **tuberculosis** on the way home.

DICK PICKERSGILL

★ **Explorer learns from Cook**

★ **Makes his own secret mission**

Dick Pickersgill sailed with Cook on his first two voyages. Like Cook, Pickersgill was a good mapmaker. On the third voyage, the Royal Navy asked Cook to look for the Northwest Passage from west to east. No one told Cook they had also sent Pickersgill to look for it from east to west. Pickersgill's expedition failed when he found his route was blocked by ice.

JOSEPH BANKS

★ **Gentleman sails onboard**

★ **Brings home native people**

Joseph Banks was a **naturalist** on Cook's first voyage. He paid for Cook to also take two more naturalists, two artists, two servants, a secretary—and two greyhounds. When they got home, Banks tried to steal the glory for the voyage's success. He wrote the first book about the voyage. Banks also had this portrait painted with a man he brought home from the Society Islands named Omai and the naturalist Daniel Solander (right).

POLYNESIAN PRIEST

☞ **Tupaia is expert navigator**

☞ **Draws Europeans a map!**

Tupaia was a Polynesian who joined Cook on the *Endeavour* as a translator. He drew Cook a detailed map of the islands of the South Pacific. Joseph Banks wanted to take Tupaia back to London. Like many of the crew, however, Tupaia died of sickness on the way home.

WILLIAM BLIGH

★ **A harsh officer**

William Bligh was an officer on Cook's third voyage. Later, he was a harsh commander on his own ship, the *Bounty*. Bligh's crew **mutinied** and abandoned him in the South Pacific. He survived, however.

Check Out the Ride

For all of his voyages, Cook used old coal ships called colliers. They were strong vessels with flat bottoms that could be navigated through shallow waters. They had lots of room for supplies.

FIRST VOYAGE

+ Cook chooses an old coal ship

For his first voyage, Cook chose a small coal ship from Whitby. It was called the *Endeavour*. Cook fitted the ship with cannons, boats for going ashore, and extra planks to make the hull sturdier. In Australia, the Great Barrier Reef ripped holes in the ship's hull, but the *Endeavour*'s flat bottom made it very stable, so it did not **capsize**. The crew used timber and sailcloth to repair the hole.

DECK DISASTER

☛ Banks's plans spell trouble

For his second voyage, Cook's ships were two more colliers, the *Resolution* and *Adventure*. The naturalist Joseph Banks planned to travel aboard the *Resolution*. He got the Navy to build an extra deck onboard, but it made the boat so top-heavy it almost tipped over. After Cook ordered the deck removed, Banks decided to stay home.

THIRD VOYAGE

★ *Resolution* refitted

★ Cook updates favorite ship

On his third voyage, Cook set out to try to find the Northwest Passage. He had the *Resolution* refitted and chose a new companion ship, the *Discovery*. Both were updated with a **forge** for making nails, an oven, and equipment to make drinking water from sea water. These upgrades meant the ships could stay at sea for longer. Cook also took special clocks that kept time accurately at sea. The clocks helped Cook work out his **longitude**, or the ship's position from east to west.

EXTRA PASSENGERS

☛ Animals onboard

Cook's ships each carried 90 to 120 men. They also carried animals such as pigs, hens, and a goat to provide meat, eggs, and milk on the voyage. It was also common for men to take pets onboard, such as dogs, cats, or monkeys. The pets helped break up the boredom of long days at sea. On Cook's third voyage, he carried some unusual animals. The British king, King George III, was an enthusiastic farmer and he asked Cook to take animals from the king's own farms as gifts for the Polynesians. The animals included sheep, rabbits, horses, two cows, a bull— and even a peacock and a peahen. The animals' pens and their food took up so much room that the sailors' quarters were more cramped than usual.

Solve It With Science

James Cook's voyages to the Pacific Ocean resulted in significant breakthroughs for science. Cook and his crew also relied on the latest scientific advances to make their long voyages possible.

SO LONG SCURVY

★ **Cook defeats sailors' disease**

★ **Uses vinegar and sauerkraut**

Many sailors on long voyages suffered from **scurvy**. This is a disease that is caused by a lack of Vitamin C. Cook made his men eat specific foods to try to prevent scurvy. These foods included sauerkraut, mustard, vinegar, and malt. He also made sure his men were clean and warm, and that the ship was dry and well aired. No one died from scurvy on his voyages—although some died from other diseases. Cook became known as the man who defeated scurvy.

A DOT ON THE SUN...

+ Explorer observes passage of Venus

The original reason for Cook's first voyage to the Pacific was to observe the transit of Venus. This happens every 243 years. As Venus passes between Earth and the Sun, it appears as a small black disk against the Sun (but don't ever look directly at the Sun, it can severely hurt your eyes). Scientists wanted to view the planet from different places on the globe. They hoped to use math to work out the distance from Earth to the Sun.

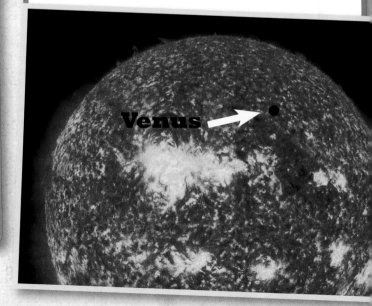

Venus →

NATIVE CHIEF SHOWS THE WAY?

☛ **Cook charts new lands**

Cook made charts of the Pacific that were so accurate that sailors were still using them in the early 20th century. Cook learned from the native peoples of the Pacific Islands. Tupaia of Tahiti helped him make a map of the many small islands that filled the southern Pacific. Tupaia's local knowledge meant that his map of the area was as accurate as most maps being made by European explorers using the latest measuring techniques and equipment.

My Explorer Journal

★ Imagine if someone like Cook asked you to draw a map of the area where you live. What do you think it would be important to include? What kind of things might you leave out?

All at Sea

The British Admiralty offered a huge reward for whoever solved the problem of longitude. John Harrison, a clockmaker, spent 30 years inventing a marine chronometer—but the Admiralty refused to pay up.

TRAVEL UPDATE

No longer a problem

If you're setting out to sail around the world, you can use the stars or the Sun to work out how far north or south you are. But to find your location east or west you need to compare the time where you are with the time it was when you set out—and unfortunately watches are inaccurate on board ships. Good news! On his second voyage, Captain Cook tested a new marine **chronometer** invented by John Harrison. It only loses a third of a second a day! With this new invention, **longitude** can now be precisely measured!

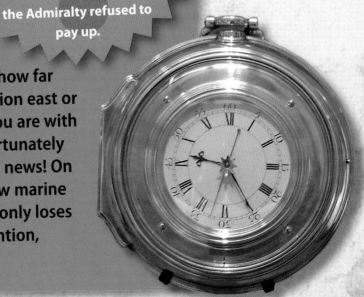

Hanging at Home

Cook and his crew visited many different places—some very hot, others extremely cold. They tried to live as comfortably as possible, both at sea and on land.

CAPTAIN'S QUARTERS

- ☛ Cook sails in comfort
- ☛ Other ranks sleep where they can

Cook's ship was his second home. He had the largest cabin onboard (right), with large windows for light. Other officers and scientists had smaller, private cabins. The sailors crowded into **hammocks** below deck. Some had to squeeze themselves into spaces in storage areas.

 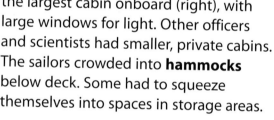

GOING TO EXTREMES!

Cook's voyages took him to the frozen seas. He and his men had to eat seals, penguins, and large seabirds known as albatross. They also journeyed through the heat of the equator. There, books went moldy and iron fittings rusted. In Tahiti, flies pestered everybody. There was an artist on board, but flies ate his paint!

TRAVEL UPDATE

Temporary wives

★ If you visited Tahiti in the 18th century, you might be offered a "temporary wife" among the local women. Some men on Cook's first voyage accepted the offer. They claimed they did not want to seem rude. Two men tried to stay behind with their Tahitian "wives." Cook forced them back on the ship.

My Explorer Journal

★ **Cook's crew visited some of the hottest and coldest places on earth. Think about being either very hot or very cold onboard a ship. Make a list of good and bad things about both. Which would you prefer? Give an explanation for your decision.**

A RECIPE FOR ALBATROSS

As they visited different places, Cook's men tried eating all sorts of animals to see how they tasted. Joseph Banks recorded this recipe for cooking an albatross: "Skin and soak in salt water overnight. Stew and serve with savoury sauce."

FURNEAUX AND OMAI

★ An exotic celebrity

Tobias Furneaux commanded HMS *Adventure* on Cook's second voyage. Furneaux met a Pacific Islander named Omai. He brought Omai back to London, where the islander became a celebrity in London society. On the third voyage, Cook returned Omai to his island home.

Meeting and Greeting

Some of the people Cook met on his travels were friendly. They helped the European navigators. Some individuals even joined the expedition themselves.

THE TAHITIANS

- ☛ Islanders welcome explorers
- ☛ Have met Europeans before

Cook arrived in Tahiti soon after the first European visitors. The Tahitians knew that Europeans had iron to trade—and that they carried guns. They were very friendly. Chief Lycurgus and his family often ate with the officers. A former queen named Obadia also spent time with Cook's crew.

THE FUEGIANS

- ★ Peoples of the far south
- ★ Captain not impressed

In Tierra del Fuego, at the southern tip of South America, Cook's men met native Fuegians. The Fuegians seemed friendly, but Cook noted that their homes were poor shelters of grass and they had no chiefs or leaders. He called them "as miserable a set of people as are this day upon Earth."

COMPETITORS!

+ European colonists welcome Cook

On his voyages, Cook visited European **colonies** around the world. He met Portuguese settlers in Brazil and Dutch settlers in Batavia, Indonesia, and in Cape Town in South Africa. People were often friendly, especially when Cook became famous after his first voyage. However, some were also wary of Cook. Their countries were competing for riches and territories—so no one wanted to give too much information away!

> The discoveries we have made, tho not great, will apologize for the length of the voyage."
> *Cook writes to the Admiralty after returning from his first voyage, 1771*

THE ALEUT AND CHUKCHI

☛ **Warm welcome in a cold land**

☛ **Natives want to trade**

The Aleut and Chukchi people of the Arctic Circle had already met Russian explorers. They had no fear of European peoples. When Cook's ships visited the Bering Strait in 1778, 21 search for the Northwest Passage, these native peoples rowed out to meet them. They were eager to trade furs for tobacco.

My Explorer Journal

★ Explorers like Cook kept logs about discovering unknown lands and people. Imagine if native peoples kept logs. How might they describe a visit by Europeans? What might they think if Cook and his men put up a strange flag, told them that they were now British subjects—and then left?

Not Too Close

Some of the people Cook met were not very friendly. Sometimes Cook's men wanted to keep their distance as well. They were frightened that the native peoples might overwhelm them.

THE MAORI OF NEW ZEALAND

☛ **Warlike hunters scare off crew**

When Cook first met the Maori of New Zealand in 1769, one of his sailors shot and killed a man before Cook was even ashore. Later, the Maori avoided the Europeans. After Cook's men learned that some Maori were **cannibals**, they kept their distance, too! Once, eleven men who went ashore from the *Adventure* to gather food were killed by a group of Maori—and eaten! Other crewmen identified their remains when they found a hand tattooed with its owner's initials.

New Zealand
The Maori of New Zealand were so warlike that Cook's men rarely went ashore. They mapped the coasts of New Zealand from onboard the ship, mainly staying safely out at sea.

TRAVEL UPDATE

Petty theft and punishment
★ If you lead an expedition like James Cook, try to treat other peoples fairly. They may not understand the idea of private property, for example, and may take things from the ships. Cook usually solved problems fairly, but by his third voyage he seemed to have less patience. Sometimes he had thieves lashed. In 1779, when Cook arrived in Hawaii, the harsh way he treated some natives caused a fight that led to Cook's death.

ABORIGINES IN AUSTRALIA

☛ Off to a bad start

Cook received a cool welcome from the Aboriginal people in Australia. At first, they simply ignored the Europeans. Later, after Cook had been in Australia for months, a few sailors caught some giant turtles. A group of natives demanded that Cook return them. Cook refused and the Aboriginal people burned down his camp. The two sides later made peace.

Did you know?

When Cook's ships first sailed into Botany Bay in Australia, the local people carried on with their lives. One family cooked and ate a meal on the shore while completely ignoring the approaching ships.

TATTOO YOU!

★ **Polynesians covered in ink**

★ **New fashion trend for sailors!**

On his first voyage, Cook and his crew met Polynesians whose bodies were so covered in tattoos they looked as if they were wearing clothes. The tattoos were signs of status that indicated the achievements of the wearer. The tattoos were created by using needles to push dye beneath the surface of the skin. Some of Cook's men got their own tattoos in Samoa. When they returned to Europe in 1771, they began a naval tradition of sailors being tattooed. The word "tattoo" comes from the Samoan "tatau."

I Love Nature

As Cook traveled to new and distant lands, he always took naturalists to study and record any new plants and animals they found.

Bag a Rat

In Tahiti, there were "swarms" of rats running over the ground. For fun, the crew shot more than 1,000 rats a day. They also reported that the rats were tasty to eat!

BOTANY BAY

★ **Banks in botanical heaven**

★ **Hundreds of new species**

On the *Endeavour's* first voyage in eastern Australia, Joseph Banks and his team found more than 1,000 species of plants and animals they had never seen before. Cook had named their landing place Stingray Harbor. Because it was home to so many new plants, however, he renamed it Botany Bay.

I NAME THEE ME

☛ **Banks names new plant after himself**

At Botany Bay, Banks was the first European to discover a plant that he named *Banksia* after himself. It was over 49 feet (15 meters) tall, with spiky flowers in yellow, orange, red, pink, and violet. Banksia is very unusual. It only releases its seeds after a bush fire. The fire leaves ash on the ground where the seeds can easily grow.

BOW WOW WOW

+ Dog tracks indicate new species

When they went ashore at Botany Bay, Joseph Banks and his fellow naturalist, Daniel Solander, recorded seeing what looked like the tracks of a dog. They belonged to a dingo, a wild dog that lives throughout most of Australia. Its name comes from the word *tingo*, the aboriginal peoples' word for dog.

TRAVEL UPDATE

Wonders of nature

★ If you're heading for the southern seas, watch out for unusual events. In New Zealand, Cook's ships dodged waterspouts, or whirling columns of air and mist. In the Antarctic, they saw the "southern lights," ghostly colors in the night sky. Cook also observed "ice blink," when bright spots appear in the sky. The spots are caused by light reflected from ice hidden out of sight beyond the horizon.

Did you know?

Near Botany Bay, Banks and his scientists discovered another new species: mudskippers. These fish use their fins to "run" across the land between bodies of water!

IS THAT DEER HOPPING?

★ Explorers meet kangaroos

Joseph Banks describes the size of a kangaroo as "not less than a deer." The sailors found this unusual **herbivore** difficult to hunt, but Banks' greyhound, Lady, was able to catch little ones.

Fortune Hunting

There were different kinds of riches at stake on Cook's voyages. Money was just one of them. Equally important were fame, knowledge, national pride, and the discovery of new territory.

FOR KING AND COUNTRY

☞ Building the empire

Britain was building a large and powerful **empire**. Cook's work helped Britain set up naval stations around the Pacific. Australia and New Zealand later became loyal colonies. If there actually was a "great southern continent," then Britain wanted to claim that, too.

POWER IS KNOWLEDGE

+ A world of wonders

Cook's voyages were a period of rich scientific discovery. On the first voyage, Banks and his team identified over 3,000 new species of plants and animals, such as black swans (left). These discoveries helped create Britain's reputation as one of the world's leading scientific nations.

PRISON COLONIES

★ **Britain sends convicts overseas**

★ **Solves problem of crowded jails**

Cook's discoveries helped Britain deal with a prisoner crisis at home. Britain's jails were full of prisoners. It had previously sent convicts to work in its American colonies, but that stopped after the United States became independent from Britain in 1776. The British government then set up prison colonies in Australia. Convicts could be transported to prison settlements such as Botany Bay or Van Dieman's Land.

Did you know?

The British government offered a reward for the discovery of the Northwest Passage. It was never claimed. The route was only traveled by the Norwegian Roald Amundsen in 1906.

BIG BUSINESS

☛ **Exploration helps business**

☛ **No route to China, claims Cook**

Whale fat was valuable in the 18th century. The oil was burned in lamps. There was a lot of money to be made in whaling—if you knew where to find whales. After Cook's voyages, whalers knew much more about where whales could be found in the southern seas. Cook was also trying to make it easier to trade with China by finding a shorter route to Asia. He failed to discover the Northwest Passage, however, so the voyage remained long and potentially dangerous.

This Isn't What It Said in the Brochure!

Cook took his men's safety very seriously. His worst moments were when they were sick or in danger—and these incidents happened quite often.

RUN AGROUND!

- ☞ Ship holed on reef
- ☞ Crew stranded for months

In 1770, as the *Endeavour* sailed up the east coast of Australia, it got stuck on the Great Barrier Reef. To try and refloat the ship, the crew threw heavy objects overboard—even the cannon. Cook was worried that waves would break the ship apart. He got his men to drag the vessel off the reef, even though it tore holes in the ship. Then he deliberately grounded the ship on a beach. The crew spent three months repairing the ship.

TRAVEL UPDATE

Disease and Death

★ On a voyage, remember that being on land can be more dangerous than being at sea. Near the end of his first voyage, Cook noted that he had not lost one man to scurvy. Then he landed in Batavia, a Dutch port in what is now Indonesia. Many sailors caught an infection. Before they got to the next port, 34 had died!

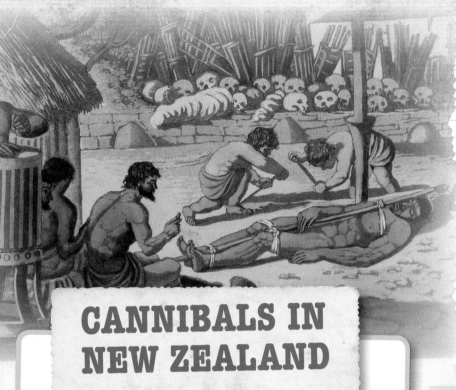

★ **Cook and his crew were stuck on the Great Barrier Reef for over two months as they repaired the *Endeavour*. They lived in a small camp on the shore, where they set up a blacksmith's forge to make nails. What else might they have needed in the camp?**

CANNIBALS IN NEW ZEALAND

+ Diet of human flesh

In New Zealand, Cook's crew learned that some Maori were cannibals. Cook wrote that their practice of eating their dead enemies was probably an ancient custom. He thought it could not be changed. But Cook's men were horrified when they found the severed head of a victim and one Maori onboard the ship began to cut and eat flesh from the head!

THE GLORY HUNTER

☛ **Joseph Banks claims the credit!**

After his first voyage, Cook almost did not get the credit for his remarkable skill as a navigator. The naturalist Joseph Banks convinced people that he had been the leader of the expedition. He said Cook had just sailed the *Endeavour*. Banks wrote books about the voyage based on Cook's journals but pretended he had made the important decisions. Banks was a leading member of London society, so people believed him. Banks refused to sail on the second voyage when Cook would not allow him to add an extra deck to the *Resolution* for his scientific equipment.

End of the Road

James Cook never completed his third voyage. On February 14, 1779, he was killed in a fight with warriors in Hawaii. The *Resolution* and *Discovery* sailed for home without their captain.

ARRIVING IN HAWAII

- ☛ Native mistake sailor for god
- ☛ Ceremonial welcome for Cook

Hawaiian islanders had never met Europeans before January 1779, when Cook arrived. The Europeans landed during a festival for the god, Orono. The Hawaiians thought Cook must be this god. King Terreeoboo filled HMS *Resolution* with food. Cook sailed away, but he returned after the ship was damaged in a storm. The Hawaiians began stealing from *Resolution* and *Discovery* and Cook began to lose his temper.

FATAL RETURN

- ★ Fatal fight on the beach
- ★ Cook killed... and cooked!

When a boat from the *Discovery* went missing on Hawaii, Cook took some crew members ashore to seize King Terreeoboo. The Hawaiians on the beach threw stones at the Europeans and the sailors began shooting. Cook and four crewmen were killed. The Hawaiians honored their enemies by cooking their bodies. They later returned Cook's bones to his crew, who buried them at sea.

THE EXPEDITION AFTER COOK

+ A failed visit to the Arctic

After Cook's death, Charles Clerke led the expedition back to the Arctic. He wanted to make one more attempt at finding the Northwest Passage. By this time, Clerke had tuberculosis. He knew that he would not make it back to England. After he died, the *Resolution* and *Discovery* sailed home under the command of John Gore.

COOK REMEMBERED

★ Monuments everywhere

Monuments and statues to Cook are dotted around the world. He gave many places the names they still have today. A lot of places are named for Cook, including the Cook Islands in the South Pacific and Mount Cook in Alaska.

A MAN OF SCIENCE

+ Enemies give Cook safe passage

In 1779, Britain and its American colonies were fighting the American Revolutionary War. The American representative in France, Benjamin Franklin, said that Cook's ships should have safe passage through American waters. He said Cook's expedition was for the good of all humankind. In fact, Cook himself had already been killed, but Franklin's gesture was later recognized with a special medal from the Royal Society in London.

GLOSSARY

aboriginal Existing in a place from the earliest times

botany The scientific study of plants

cannibals People who eat the flesh of other humans

capsizing Tipping over of a boat

chronometer A very acccurate watch or clock for keeping time at sea

colonies Distant lands under the control of another country

collier A ship built to carry coal

coral A hard, stoneline substance made from the skeletons of many thousands of tiny sea creatures

empire A number of lands under one ruler

forge An oven for heating metal to make if soft, so that it can be shaped

herbivore An animal that mainly eats plants

hammocks Nets used for sleeping that are slung between two points

labyrinth A maze

longitude A measure of distance east or west of the prime meridian in Greenwich, England

mutinied Rebelled against the captain or officer in charge

naturalists A word used in the 1700s for scientists who study nature, such as botanists or zoologists

navigation Directing travel by figuring out location, route, and distance traveled

Northwest Passage A sea route through the Canadian Arctic from the Atlantic Ocean to the Pacific Ocean

ranks Different levels of seniority in the armed forces

scurvy A disease caused by lack of Vitamin C that results in loss of teeth, joint stiffness, loss of memory, and sometimes death

surveyors People who examine and map the size and shape of land

transit A journey across, over, or through something

tuberculosis A disease caused by bacteria in the lungs

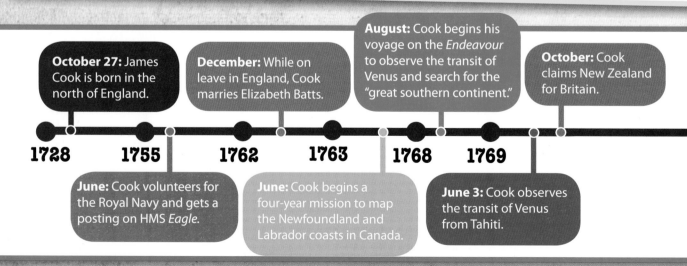

October 27: James Cook is born in the north of England.

December: While on leave in England, Cook marries Elizabeth Batts.

August: Cook begins his voyage on the *Endeavour* to observe the transit of Venus and search for the "great southern continent."

October: Cook claims New Zealand for Britain.

1728   **1755**   **1762**   **1763**   **1768**   **1769**

June: Cook volunteers for the Royal Navy and gets a posting on HMS *Eagle.*

June: Cook begins a four-year mission to map the Newfoundland and Labrador coasts in Canada.

June 3: Cook observes the transit of Venus from Tahiti.

ON THE WEB

http://southseas.nla.gov.au/index_maps.html
Clickable map of the *Endeavour* voyage with links to Cook's daily journal entries.

www.captcook-ne.co.uk
Captain Cook's Birthplace Museum. Website includes quizzes, activities, and recipes.

www.cookmuseumwhitby.co.uk/captain-cook
Information on Cook's life and voyages, including countries with links to Cook.

http://thecanadianencyclopedia.ca/en/article/james-cook/
Information from Historica Canada with links to related articles.

http://schools-wikipedia.org/wp/j/James_Cook.htm
A student-friendly teaching resource prepared by SOS Children.

BOOKS

Beales, R.A. *James Cook: The Pacific Coast and Beyond* (In the Footsteps of Explorers). Crabtree Publishing, 2006.

Bingham, Jane. *Captain Cook's Pacific Explorations* (Great Journeys Across Earth). Heinemann, 2008.

Feinstein, Stephen. *Captain Cook: Great Explorer of the Pacific* (Great Explorers of the World). Enslow Publishers, 2010.

Ollhoff, Jim. *Captain Cook* (Great Explorers). Abdo and Daughters, 2013.

April: Cook claims New South Wales in eastern Australia for Britain.

January 17: Cook's ships become the first to cross into the Antarctic Circle.

February 14: Cook and four of his crew are killed in a fight on the beach in Hawaii.

1770 **1772** **1773** **1776** **1778** **1779**

July 13: Cook begins his second voyage. He sails on the *Resolution* to search the Southern Hemisphere for the "great southern continent."

June 25: Cook begins his third voyage. He sets out on the *Resolution* to look for the Northwest Passage.

January 18: Cook discovers the islands of Hawaii.

INDEX

31901056943980